ARTHURIAN CAERLEON

In Literature and Legend

Chris Barber

BLORENGE
•BOOKS•

Abergavenny, Gwent
1996

First Published 1996

ISBN 1 872730 10 8

© Chris Barber

Blorenge Cottage, Church Lane, Llanfoist
Abergavenny, Gwent, NP7 9NG. Tel: 01873 856114

Printed by A PRINT,
Unit 23, Enterprise Way,
Newport, Gwent NP9 2AQ
Tel: 01633 264815

'Arthur was accustomed to hold his court at Caerleon upon Usk. And there he held it seven Easters and five Christmasses. And once upon a time he held his court there at Whitsuntide. For Caerleon was the place most easy of access in his dominions, both by land and sea.'

From the *Mabinogion* story of
'Geraint the son of Erbin'

King Arthur and his Knights of the Round Table

CONTENTS

KING ARTHUR'S PLENARY COURT AT CAERLEON

Half a century after the Romans departed from these islands, where they had been masters for nearly four hundred years, King Arthur is reputed to have held a court at Caerleon in Gwent. Such a tradition was firmly established by a Benedictine monk known as Geoffrey of Monmouth. His full name was Geoffrey ap Arthur and he became Archdeacon of Monmouth in 1151. His famous book entitled *Historia Regum Britanniae* ('A History of the Kings of Britain') was completed in 1136 and is said to be based on the translation of a Celtic manuscript discovered in Brittany. It was first translated from Latin into English in 1718 by Aaron Thompson. Historia Regum Britanniae became a twelfth century best seller and it survives in two hundred manuscripts. By the end of the twelfth century the story of Arthur was known in France, Spain, Italy, Poland and Byzantium.

Geoffrey of Monmouth has been described as ' *the most delightful old liar who ever wove historical lore out of his inner consciousness* '. However, although the book is muddled and confusing, had not this romantic history not been written then there would have been no *Idylls of the King* (written by Alfred Lord Tennyson) or *Le Morte d' Arthur* by Malory. In fact the life of Arthur would probably have been recorded as a very minor matter or perhaps even ignored completely. Geoffrey devotes one fifth of his book to the story of Arthur and makes it colourful and exciting, basing much of his information no doubt on the songs of twelfth century minstrels and the tales of the *Mabinogion*..

In every corner of Britain one encounters stories of King Arthur and an enormous number of books have been written about the subject, some even questioning his very existence. His name has been given to a wide assortment of land features - standing stones, cromlechs and rock formations throughout Britain, with Wales especially having its fair share of Arthurian curiosities.

Caerleon-upon-Usk in Gwent was once a place of considerable importance with a remarkable past, but sadly it is now generally regarded as nothing more than a suburb of sprawling Newport. Visitors come to Caerleon from far and wide seeking an Arthurian experience, fully expecting to find information relating to the Dark Age King but they are disappointed for the museum is only concerned with the story of the Roman occupation. Yet to those with romantic ideals, King Arthur is the soul of Caerleon and the subject of a long established tradition associated with this ancient place, that has been told and retold by writers and poets through the centuries.

It was Geoffrey of Monmouth's detailed description of Arthur's supposed court at Caerleon which inspired the idea of a Camelot - the capital of Arthur's kingdom. Not that Geoffrey used such a name, but he did bring Caerleon into his 'History' no less than thirteen times. Living just 20 miles away at Monmouth he had no doubt ridden the Roman road to Isca (Caerleon) and visited the impressive ruins of the old fortress.

Geoffrey tells us that after his first Gallic campaign, Arthur held a plenary court at Caerleon, which was attended by the earls and barons of the kingdoms, the vassal kings of Wales, Scotland, Cornwall, Brittany, of the conquered islands and the European provinces.

'When the feast of Whitsuntide began to draw near, Arthur, who was quite overjoyed by his great success, made up his mind to hold a plenary court at that season and place the crown of the kingdom on his head. He decided too, to summon to this feast the leaders who owed him homage, so that he could celebrate Whitsun with greater reverence and renew the closest possible pacts of peace with his chieftains. He explained to the members of his court what he was proposing to do and accepted their advice that he should carry out his plan in the City of the Legions.

Situated as it is in Glamorgan (known as Morgannwg in Geoffrey's time and later Monmouthshire), on the River Usk, not far from the Severn Sea, in a most pleasant position, and being richer in material wealth than other townships, this city was eminently suitable for such a ceremony. The river which I have named flowed by it on one side, and up this the kings and princes who were to come from across the sea could be carried in a fleet of ships. On the other side, which was flanked by meadows and wooded groves, they had adorned the city with royal palaces, and by the gold-painted gables of its roofs it was a match for Rome. What is more, it was famous for its two churches.

Caerleon upon Usk

8

One of these, built in honour of the martyr Julius, was graced by a choir of most lovely virgins dedicated to God. The second, founded in the name of the blessed Aaron, the companion of Julius, was served by a monastery of canons, and counted the third metropolitan see of Britain. The city also contained a college of two hundred learned men, who were skilled in astronomy and the other arts and so by their careful computations prophesied for King Arthur any Prodigies due at that time.

It was this city, therefore, famous for such a wealth of pleasant things, which made ready for the feast. Messengers were sent to the different kingdoms and invitations delivered to all those who were due to come to this court from the various parts of Gaul and from the nearby Islands in the Sea.'

It would seem that Geoffrey's description of a great feast at Caerleon was based on an important Christmas feast held by King Stephen at Lincoln, when the King wore his crown to go to mass. Geoffrey obviously saw Arthur's feast conducted on twelfth-century lines with a feudal homaging, a banquet and tournament in honour of the Ladies. It is indeed a fact that the ancient monarchs of France and England had a custom of holding a plenary court at the three principal festivals of Easter, Whitsuntide and Christmas.

Geoffrey of Monmouth's *Historia Regum Brittaniae* was written in about 1136 and the earliest reference to it can be found in the writings of Henry of Huntingdon who was shown the work in January 1139 when he visited the Abbey of Bec in Normandy. He referred to it as *'the big book of Geoffrey Artur'*.

It is of interest that Geoffrey dedicated his book to Robert of Gloucester the illegitimate son of Henry I by Nest the daughter of Rhys ap Tewdwr, Prince of Glamorgan. Robert, Earl of Gloucester was Lord of the Gwent Marches where Caerleon-upon-Usk is situated and he stands out among the Norman Lords on account of the encouragement he gave to the intellectual movement in Wales during the twelfth century. He was not only a soldier and a statesman, but he was also a patron of the arts and in his court he gathered a brilliant body of learned men and letters. In this company no one was more honoured than Geoffrey of Monmouth.

The appearance of Geoffrey's book caused quite a stir and it started a new epoch in literature, opening for all Europe the previously unknown and inexhaustible well of Celtic romance. Its influence upon literature and ideas has been felt in every age, inspiring some of the greatest poets with the spirit and materials for their compositions. Undoubtedly the traditions of King Arthur, set down in the romantic pages of the twelfth century, have captivated the greatest writers, from Malory, Spencer, Milton and Shakespeare to Wordsworth, Gibbon, Matthew Arnold, Tennyson, William Morris, John Masefield and others, supplying them with material for their enduring work. The story of King Arthur and the Knights of the Round Table is part of our national heritage and it should be remembered that it was through Geoffrey of Monmouth that it captured the imagination of Europe.

Fifty years after the appearance of Geoffey's 'Historia', Giraldus Cambrensis in 1187 was accompanying Baldwin the Archbishop of Canterbury on a tour of Wales, preaching the Third Crusade. They stayed one night at Casnewydd (now called Newport) and Giraldus in his 'Itinerary' speaks of that settlement as Novus Burgas or New Town to distinguish it from Caerleon, which he describes in glowing terms:-

'The city was handsomely built of masonry, with courses of bricks, by the Romans. Many vestiges of its former splendour may yet be seen, immense palaces, formerly ornamented with gilded roofs, in imitation of Roman magnificence...a town of prodigious sixe, wonderful bath-buildings, the remains of temples and theatres, all enclosed within fine walls which are yet partly standing...subterraneous buildings, water pipes, and underground passages and, more remarkable than all, stoves contrived with wonderful art to transmit the heat insensibly through narrow flues passing up the side of the walls '.

King Arthur's Round Table

THE ROUND TABLE

Giraldus Cambrensis surprisingly makes no special mention, though he doubtless saw, the still imposing remains of the Roman ampitheatre which, over 1,100 years earlier, had been built by the soldiers of the Second Legion Augusta just outside their fortress whose walls lie buried beneath the modern village of Caerleon.

People at one time used to visit Caerleon in large numbers just to see the site of 'King Arthur's Round Table' which was of course in reality the grass covered Roman ampitheatre. Locals would proudly direct the visitors to a large circular hollow in a meadow, which from the fourteenth century seems to have been known as King Arthur's Mead. It was firmly believed that the cup-shaped hollow was the scene of the Arthurian tournaments and joustings described by Sir Thomas Malory and Alfred Lord Tennyson.

The Roman ampitheatre at Caerleon

In 1926-7 the well known archaeologist, Mortimer Wheeler carried out a major excavation on this site, involving a large body of workmen, two horses and a complicated railway system. Some 30,000 tons of earth were removed to reveal the finest example of a Roman ampitheatre in Britain. It was built at about the same time as the Rome Colloseum in 80 AD and was large enough to accomodate 6,000 spectators - the entire garrison of the Roman fort of Isca.

During this period, Christians were being martyred all over the Roman Empire and in the Colloseum at Rome in particular, hundreds of Christians faced death for their faith. It is quite likely that many such believers, suffered a cruel death in the arena of the Caerleon ampitheatre.

Gildas, writing in the sixth-century asserts that Caerleon was the site of the first Christian martyrdom in Britain and it is of interest that an excavation here in 1929 revealed the earliest evidence of Christianity in Britain. An antifex or an ornamental tile was discovered, on which in place of the customary design to represent the sun, was carved a cross.

One tends to think of Christians being thrown to the lions and we are told by certain monk-historians of the time that when persecution under the Emperor Diocletian in 303 was carried out, two of the inhabitants of Caerleon, Julius and Aaron were among the earliest British martyrs. They are said to have been 'torn to pieces' and they perhaps perished in combat with wild animals in the ampitheatre. Bede, writing in the 7th century, certainly speaks of their martyrdom taking place in Caerleon and in their memory, two churches were later established and dedicated to them.

Geoffrey of Monmouth states that the City of the Legions *was famous for its two churches, one of these, built in honour of the martyr Julius, was graced by a choir of the most lovely virgins dedicated to God. The second, founded in the name of the blessed Aaron, the companion of Julius, was served by a monastery of canons, and counted as the third metropolitan see of Britain.'*

We are also told by Geoffrey that just before the battle of Camlan, *'Queen Guinevere gave way to despair. She fled to the City of the Legions and there, in the church of Julius the Martyr, she took her vows among the nuns, promising to lead a chaste life.'*

MARTYRIUMS FOR JULIUS AND AARON

The site of the church of Julius the Martyr, where Geoffrey claims that Queen Guinevere became a nun is believed to have been about a mile to the west of Caerleon, close to an Elizabethan mansion known as St Julians. The mansion was unfortunately demolished in the 1970s but it was reputed to occupy the site of some monastic buildings, which echoed the tradition that here once stood the church dedicated to the martyr Julius.

Aaron, the companion of Julius, who was also martyred at the same time (1 July 303), was according to local tradition buried at Penrhos to the north-east of Caerleon, where a chapel was erected to his memory on the site of a small Roman camp, constructed as an outpost to the Legionary fortress.

SAINTS DYFRIG AND DEWI

Geoffrey of Monmouth also speaks of a metropolitan church at Caerleon and he developed the story that this was the seat of an Archbishop and claimed that St Dyfrig (Dubricius), who crowned Arthur, was one of those who occupied the archiepiscopal throne here. However, it is more likely that Dyfrig was appointed Bishop of Caerleon for there was no archbishop in Britain in those days.

Geoffrey also tells us that Dyfrig was Principal of a college here where *astronomy and other arts were taught by 200 learned men, and it was the responsibility of the astronomers to predict Arthur's future.*

It was a custom of the clergy to follow their countrymen to the battlefield when the cause of combat was a natural and just one, in order to rouse the courage of the soldiers and pray for them during the struggle. Geoffrey of Monmouth states that St Dyfrig the 'Archbishop' of Caerleon followed Arthur to Bath, to be present at the battle of Badon and that he addressed the soldiers before the combat to give them encouragement.

Dyfrig in due course resigned his position and took leave of his bretheren to seek solitude on Ynys Enlli (Bardsey Island) where he led a hermit's life - fasting and praying to the day of his death. In 1120 his remains were removed from the island by Urban, Bishop of Llandaff and re-interred in the church of Llandaff on 23 May of that year.

St Dyfrig was followed by St Dewi as 'Archbishop' of Caerleon. He is supposed to have accepted the position with reluctance but took up residence and remained there for several years. We are told that he then obtained the consent of King Arthur to remove the See from Caerleon to Menevia (in West Wales), the place of his birth.

It would seem that Dewi not only transferred his episcopal seat from Caerleon, but also the renowned school, or college established and superintended by Dyfrig. The reason for this transfer to the far west was no doubt as a result of concern over the advances of the dreaded

Saxons. Some years later King Morgan Mwynfawr is also said to have moved his court away from Caerleon, first to Rhadyr, near Cardiff and then to Margam, near Port Talbot.

THE THIRTEEN TREASURES OF THE ISLAND OF BRITAIN

There is a tradition recorded in ancient literature that the 'Thirteen rarieties of Kingly Regalia of the Island of Britain were formerly kept at Caerleon, on the River Usk, in Monmouthshire.' These curiosities we are told went with Myrddin (Merlin), the son of Movran, into the House of Glass, in Enlli, or Bardsey Island. Other writers tell us that it was Taliesin, the chief of the bards, who possessed them and according to one old manuscript the thirteen treasures were as follows:-

1. Dyrwyn, the sword of Rhydderch Hael; if any man drew it except himself, it burst into a flame from the cross to the point, and all who asked it received it; but because of this property all shunned it; and therefore was he called Rhydderch Hael.

2. The basket of Gwyddno Garanhir; if food for man were put into it, when opened it would be found to contain food for one hundred.

3. The horn of Bran Galed; what liquor soever was desired was found therein.

4. The chariot of Morgan Mwynfawr; whoever sat in it would be immediately taken wheresoever he desired.

5. The halter of Clydno Eiddyn; which was in a staple below the feet of his bed, and whatever horse he wished for in it he would find there.

6. The knife of Llawfrodedd Farchawg; which would serve four-and-twenty men at meat all at once.

7. The couldron of Tyrnog; if meat were put in it to boil for a coward it would never be boiled, but if meat were put in it for a brave man it would be boiled forthwith.

The whetstone of Tudwal Tudclud; if the sword of a brave man were sharpened thereon and anyone were wounded therewith he would be sure to die, but if it were that of a coward that was sharpened on it he would be none the worse.

9, The garment of Padarn Beisrudd; if a man of gentle birth put it on, it suited him well, but of a churl it would not fit him.

10, 11. The pan and the platter of Rhegynydd Ysgolbaig; whatever food was required was found therein.

12. The chess board of Gwenddolen; when the men were placed upon it, they would play themselves. The chess board was of gold, and the men of silver.

13. The mantle of Arthur; whosoever was beneath it could see everything, while no one could see him.'

ST HENWG AND TALIESIN THE BARD

Just outside Caerleon, perched on the end of a narrow ridge, providing extensive views is the hamlet of Llanhennock where the first church established here was dedicated to St Henwg. The tradition is that it was founded by the Arthurian bard, Taliesin in memory of his father. An 18th century manuscript compiled by Thomas Hopkin of Coychurch gives the pedigree of Taliesin as follows:-

Taliesin, Chief of Bards of the West, the son of Henwg the Bard of the College of Saint Cadocus, the son of Flwch Ladwrwm, of Caerleon upon Usk, the son of Cynvar, the son of Saint Clydog, the son of Gwynnor, the son of Cadrain, the son of Caradog, the son of Bran the Blessed, the son of Llyr Llediath.

There is a tradition that Henwg went to Rome on a mission to Constantine the Blessed requesting that he would send Saints Germanus and Lupus to Britain, to strengthen the faith and renew baptism.

Taliesin the 'Radiant Brow' we are told was invited by Arthur to his court at Caerleon-upon-Usk, *'where he became highly celebrated for poetic genius and useful, meretorious sciences.'* His name is also commemorated in the Welsh Triads :-

'The three Baptismal Bards of the Isle of Britain:-
Myrddin Emrys, Taliesin, Chief of Bards and Myrddin son of Madoc Morfryn.'

Taliesin's *'feats, learning and endowments were found to be so superior that he was created a golden-tongued knight of the Round Table.'*

After the abdication of Arthur, Taliesin became Chief Bard to Urien Gorre, at Aberllychwr, who has been confused with Urien Rheged. He can be identified with Urbgennius, the Consul de Badon of Geoffrey's 'Historia' who is said to have attended the crown-wearing ceremony of King Arthur held at Caerleon, where a great celebration was held on the feast day of St Aaron. There is also a tradition that Urien was buried in the coronation chapel of St Aaron.

The Church of St Cadoc, Caerleon

THE CADOC CONNECTION

Standing in the centre of Caerleon is the Parish Church of Llangattock-juxta-Caerleon, which is dedicated to St Cadoc who was another contemporary of King Arthur. In the Life of St Cadoc we are told that a brave leader of the Britons, Ligessaw Lawhir (Longhand), son of Elimon, had killed three soldiers of Arthur. When Arthur was told, he tracked the murderer from place to place and the man unable to find safety elsewhere, came as a fugitive to Cadoc, to whom he confessed his sin and told his danger. The Abbot received him into his monastery, though some of the bretheren dissented, on the plea that to do so would draw down upon them the wrath of the king.

Ligessaw remained with the monks for seven years, when someone revealed his place of refuge to Arthur, who despatched messengers to Llancarfan to demand his expulsion. When Cadoc refused to surrender Llyngesog, the king became very indignant. But he refrained from actual violence, through a kind of religious fear, for people spoke of Cadoc as being guarded by angels from heaven, and of the woe of attending those who molested him.

After much negotiation between the King and the Abbot, it was agreed that the matter should be submitted to arbitration. David, Teilo, Oudoceus and others defended Cadoc. The judges assembled on the banks of the river Usk, and the subject was so warmly discussed, and the excitement so intense, that it seemed judicious that the adherents of each party should keep the river between them.

At last it was decreed that Arthur should receive three 'best oxen' for the redemption of each of his three slain soldiers. When agreement was reached, Arthur turned awkward, saying that he would only have cows, which were red in the front and white in the rear. But where could such cows be found? St Cadoc told his men to drive up before him nine or (as some say) a hundred heifers, of whatever colour they might be, which were immediately changed by God at the saint's request into the coloures desired by Arthur.

The judges then decided that St Cadoc should drive the cows into the middle of the ford, whilst Arthur, Cai and Bedwyr should there receive them, all sitting still. When Cai and Bedwyr drew them in by their horns, they were miraculously transformed into bundles of ferns. Arthur then became penitent, and the cows were soon afterwards found safe in the stalls of their owners.

The story ends with a grand reconciliation. Arthur bestows rights of sanctuary upon St Cadoc extending over seven years, seven months and seven days. Also should any stranger under Cadoc's protection set sail from sanctuary and be driven back by bad weather to St Cadoc's harbour and return to his original sanctuary, he was to remain henceforth in safety till death

The place where all this occured is said to be Tredunnock, which is derived from Trefedinauc which means 'The town of fern', whilst the ford over the Usk, where the two parties argued was called Rhyd Gwrthebau ('the Ford of Rejoinders').

St Cadoc is also mentioned in the Welsh Triads as having a connection with King Arthur's Court, as one of its 'three wisest counsellors' and one of the three keepers of the Holy Grail.

Tredunnock Church

NOTED BY NENNIUS

The oldest historical document in which Arthur is mentioned by name is the *Historia Brittonum* which is ascribed to Nennius. Parts of this work may heve been put together as early as the seventh century, but the compilation, as we now have it was due to a certain Nennius (Nyniau) who lived about the year 800.

It may be roughly divided into two parts with the first, of sixty-six sections or chapters, professing to give a cursory sketch of the history of Britain from the earliest times down to the eigth century; the second containing a list of 'cities of Britain', together with an account of certain 'marvels' (Mirabilia), or wonderful natural phenomena, of Britain, which the compiler tells us, he '*wrote as other scribes had done before him.*'

The quasi-historical part of the work contains the fullest account of Arthur's military exploits to be found in any chronicle before that of Geoffrey of Monmouth, while from the sundry allusions to Arthur in the section on'the marvels of Britain', we gather that legend was already busy with his name.

A brief account of twelve battle fought by Arthur is given including 'the ninth battle fought at the City of the Legion'. Some Arthurian scholars argue that this may have been at Chester (where the Twentieth Legion was situated), but there is however a much dtronger case for it having taken place at Caerleon upon Usk.

MENTIONED IN THE MABINOGION

Caerleon is mentioned several times in the Mabinogion which is a collection of Welsh bardic tales originally contained in the 14th century Red Book of Hergest and said to have been written in South Wales between 1373 and 1425. They were translated into English by Lady Charlotte Guest in 1838. The form in which they have been handed down to us is not later than the fourteenth or fifteenth century but they existed in oral form however, many ages before this date and were originally told at the fireside, to while away the time and to cultivate the feeling of chivalry.. They were handed down from one generation to another and no doubt subjected to modifications.

It was at Caerleon that, according to the Mabinogion, King Arthur was sitting '*on a seat of green rushes, over the same a covering of flame-coloured satin, and a cushion of red satin under his elbow,* ' in company with Owain, and Kynon, and Kai, and with Queen Gwenhyvar and her handmaidens at work hard by when Kynon told of his wonderful discovery. He had found the fairest valley in the world, containing a fair castle where he was hospitably entertained by twenty-four maidens, the least comely of whom was fairer than even Arthur's Queen. He told how he saw the fairy fountain and the mystic stone beside it; how a tremendous storm arose when he cast water on the stone; and how came forth a black knight with whom he did battle.

In the story '*Peredur, the son of Evrawc,*' King Arthur is represented as holding his courts at Caerleon, when Peredur came thither and was most grossly insulted by Kai, the sewer or controller of the household.

It was to Caerleon that Sir Peredur returned after killing the Addanc (a monster of the lake), and where he was visited by the Black Maiden who was described as follows:-

'*Blacker were her face and her two hands than the blackest iron covered with pitch, and her hue was not more frightful than her form. High cheek bones had she, and a face lengthened downwards, and a short nose with distended nostrils. And one eye was of a piercing mottled grey, and the other was as black as jet, deep sunk in her head. And her teeth were long and yellow, more yellow were they than the flower of the broom. And her stomach rose from the breast bone higher than her chin, and her back was in the shape of a crook, and her legs were large and bony. And her figure was very thin and spare, except her feet and legs which were of huge size.*' Can the imagination conceive a more horrible female? Yet there were even greater horrors to be encountered in the neighbourhood.

The Coronation of Arthur

23

According to the story of *'Geraint and Erbin'*, Arthur held court at Caerleon through seven Easters and five Christmases and on one occasion at Whitsuntide, for: *'it was the most accessible place in his dominions, by sea and by land. And there were assembled nine crowned kings, who were his tributaries, and likewise earls and barons. For they were his invited guests at all the high festivals, unless they were prevented by any great hindrance. An when he was at Caerlleon, holding his court, thirteen churches were set apart for mass. And thus were they appointed: one church for Arthur and his Kings, and his guests; and the second for Gwenhwyfar and her ladies; and the third for the Steward of the Household and the suitors; and the fourth for the Franks and the other officers; and the other nine churches were for the nine Masters of the Household.'*

Also mentioned is the royal forest of Wentwood which overlooks Caerleon. Here Arthur gave chase to the wondeful deer with the golden hoofs and golden horns. We are told how the knight Peredeur in his adventures of the Fairy Fountain rode up a ridge into this extensive forest which once stretched from the Usk at Caerleon to the Wye at Chepstow, dividing Upper Gwent from Lower Gwent.

In the story of '*The Twrch Trwyth*,' Arthur and his knights hunt the enchanted king who has taken the form of a wild boar, across Gwent from the Brecon Beacons to Abergwy (the mouth of the Wye, near Chepstow), where the creature plunges into the Severn.

The story of '*The Dream of Rhonabwy* ' is remarkable for the wonderful descriptions of Royal and knightly dress and other belongings, and desribes the fine carpet or robe called Gwenn, another of the 'Thirteen Royal Rarieties,' preserved at Caerleon :- '*A carpet of diapered satin, with an apple of ruddy gold at each corner thereof... Whoever was upon it, no one could see him, and he could see everyone.*'

When we read '*Pwll, Prince of Dyfed* ' we learn how the lost child Pryderi, is discovered outside the stable of Ternyon Twyrv Vilant (Teyrnon of the rustling fine linen). A short distance to the north-west of Caerleon is Llantarnam which is a name derived from Nant Teyrnon and the location was originally called Ynys nant Teyrnon (the island by the brook of Teyrnon). In the Mabinogion, Teyrnon is mentioned as the Lord of Gwent Iscoed and is described as the best man in the world. and is called in full Teyrnon Twryf Vilant (Teyrnon of the rustling fine linen).

25

In the final story of '*Taliesin*,' 'we are told that the great poet was the son of Henwg of Caerleon, and that he became Chief Bard of Arthur's Royal Court at Caerleon.

All these stories are much too long to allow even summaries of them to be given here; but they are wonderfully descriptive and well worth reading.

FEATURED IN THE WELSH TRIADS

The Welsh Triads are an invaluable work of reference for anyone interested in the early Welsh traditions relating to the Arthurian period. They give us the oldest account of Arthur and have come down to us in MSS which date from the twelfth to the end of the thirteenth century and translations of them can be found in '*The Four Ancient Books of Wales* '. Thirteen of the surviving triads mention Arthur and another ten feature his principal court, while two relate to his wife Gwenhwyfar (Guinevere).

Triad 64:

'The three enthroned tribes of Britain
One at Caerleon upon Usk where Arthur was supreme King, St Dewi
(David) was archbishop and Maelgwyn Gwynedd was Chief Elder.
The second at Gelliwig, where Arthur was supreme King and Bedwini
was archbishop and Caradoc Freichfras was Chief Elder.'

In another Triad we are told that:
' There were three principal festivals, Christmas, Easter and
Whitsunday which were all celebrated with joy, particularly at the
three courts of Arthur, at Caerleon on Usk in Cymru, and at Gelliwig
in Cerniw and Penryn Rhionydd in the North.'

MALORY, CHURCHYARD AND TENNYSON

The stories of King Arthur did not appear in the English language
until 1485 when William Caxton printed, as one of his first books, Sir
Thomas Malory's 'Morte d'Arthur'. This prose work is divided into
numerous short sections and Malory mentions Caerleon many times.
The Court of King Arthur moves between Cornwall and Wales, but
the author states that Caerleon was the scene of Arthur's coronation:

'...then the king moved into Wales, and let cry a great feast that it
should be holden at Pentecost after the incoronation of him at the city
of Carlion.'

Caxton in his preface to ' Le Morte d' Arthur' reinforced the idea of
a Camelot which he refers to has being in Wales and describes the
ruins of a city that were still standing: *'in Camelot, the great stones*
and the marvellous works of iron lying under ground, and royal vaults
which divers now living have seen.' He seems to be referring to
Caerleon or Caerwent, but the statement of Caxton is contradicted by
Malory himself who places Camelot at Winchester.

The sixteenth-century poet, Thomas Churchyard, wrote at some length on the Arthurian legend and in his poem *'The Worthiness of Wales '* he gives a lengthy description of Caerleon, which he says is 'now of little worth'. He asks the gods to help his pen to describe the place where King Arthur's golden hall had been and it becomes obvious through his writing that he firmly believed Geoffrey of Monmouth's story of Arthur having his court at Caerleon. He describes Arthur's crowning ceremony:

'King Arthur sure was crowned there,
*   It was his royall seate:*
And in this towne did sceptre beare,
*   With pompe and honour greate.'*

He tells of Caerleon Castle:-

'As men may muse of to behold,
But chiefly for to note:
There is a castle very old,
That may not be forgot.

It stands upon a forced hill,
Not farre from flowing flood:
Where loe ye view long vales at will
Envoyron'd with wood

A seate for any king alive,
The soyle it is so sweete:
Fresh springs doth streames of water drive
Almost through every streate.'

He then continues with slightly different verse forms to praise the landscape around Caerleon which all *'showes that most pleasures under sunne Caerleon had alone '*.

In the margins of his poem Churchyard added some notes and the most interesting of these refers to the ampitheatre: '*A deep and large round peece of ground shewes where Arthur sate* '. Churchyard was obviously convinced by Geoffrey's tale of Arthur's court in Caerleon and this was generally believed by everyone at that time.

The Hanbury Arms

On the side of the old quay at Caerleon is a quaintly built inn known as the Hanbury Arms. It is the oldest public house in the village and was built in the 15th century by a member of the Morgan family on the site of an earlier building established by the prosperous monks of Llantarnam Abbey. After 1720 it became associated with the Hanbury family during the establishment of their local tinplate industry.

29

Literary history continued on the 16 September 1856 when a stranger arrived in Caerleon and rented a room at this riverside inn. Some years later, a local chronicler, J. Cummings Walters recalled that the man:-

'...quiet and unobtrusive to a degree, soon attracted attentention from his very reserved and secluded habits. Day after day passed, and his figure was seldom seen. Frequently he would leave the house early in the morning, and go no one knew whither, and on his return partake of slight refreshment and retire to his room until next morning. It was soon recognised that the stranger was fond of long walks, and there was not a hill in the neighbourhood up whose sides he did not climb.

For a time no one took any notice of him, but occasionally a letter arriving at the post office was delivered to him. At first the name attracted no attention, but at length, Alfred Tennyson Esq.'Inscribed on successive missives, seemed to have a special interest for the local postmaster. He repeated the name until its familiarity led him to suspect that the stranger was no other than the Poet Laureate, and this ultimately proved correct.

When it became generally known that Tennyson was staying at Caerleon, visitors frequently called upon him, but he endeavoured to maintain his seclusion. '

Tennyson was a moody, reticent man who cared little for local society. He had come to Caerleon in search of atmosphere for his great work, the *Idyls of the King* and no doubt had no desire to indulge in idle conversation. He rambled, solitary from morning to night over the legend-hallowed hills and then returned to spend the evenings in his little room, thinking and jotting down the germs of his verses. From Caerleon he made expeditions to Caerphilly, Merthyr Tydfil and Raglan. With the help of local schoolmasters he learned some Welsh and endeavoured to read the Hanes Cymru (Welsh History), and the poetry of Llywarch Hen. His main source of knowledge of the Arthurian legends was Malory and the Mabinogion, which Lady Charlotte Guest had translated in 1838, but he also researched all the available histories and his writings certainly indicate a detailed knowledge of the medieval texts. Tennyson's *Idyls of the King* published in its earliest form in 1859 is a rare example of poetry as a best seller.

For years after, some of the locals remembered the poet staying there, and the chair which he chiefly occupied in his apartment was pointed to with pride.

It is the 'Tennyson window' in the Magistrates room that attracts most visitors. Set on an external projection that rises from ground level, it remains as it was in Tennyson's days. Here in 1856, Tennyson sat gazing out of the window acoss the river towards the mysterious forest of Gwent (Wentwood) and wrote:

The Usk murmus by the windows and I sit like King Arthur at Caerleon. This is a most quiet, half-ruined village of about 1500 inhabitants.'

For a long time after the room where Tennyson had slept was kept untouched, unaltered, just as if it was a 'sacred relic'. The old four poster bed used by the Poet Laureate during his stay remained there for many years afterwards.

There was a time when thousands of visitors flocked to the Hanbury Arms every summer just to see the chair where the poet sat, the table on which he wrote and the bed on which he slept. Americans in particular made the pilgrimage. They demanded to sleep in Tennyson's bed and in vain offered tempting large sums of money to the landlord for the poet's chair and the little round table, longing to carry them back across the Atlantic. To sit in the chair of Tennyson was considered an even greater attraction than to tread in the footsteps of King Arthur!

Tennyson's Window in the 'Magistrates' room in the Hanbury Arms.

THE MIGHTY MOUND AND THE GIGANTIC TOWER

One of Caerleon's most fascinating curiosities is an impressive steep-sided conical mound which is about 16 metres high and has a base circumference of 224 metres. There are numerous legends associated with this man made heap of earth and stones and it has variously been claimed to be a victory mound, the tumulus of a chief or the site of a 'gigantic tower' built by King Arthur andeven his burial place.

This was the tower that Tennyson tells us Guinevere climbed three times when she was looking for the return of Geraint and Enid across the river Usk.

'Now thrice that morning Guinevere had climb'd
The giant tower (of Caerleon) from whose high crest they say Men
saw the goodly hills of Somerset...'

THE MYNDE
CAERLEON.

The Rev Archdeacon Coxe came here during his famous tour of Monmouthshire in 1799 and learned from a local man:

'The late Mr Morgan told Mr Evans that his father (in law) as a boy, at the end of the last century (17th) could mount to the summit of a tower on the mound, and could see from thence the hills of Somerset over the Severn. His name was Walter Norman and he died extremely old in 1762.'

Coxe also observed that in the middle of the last century (17th) the tower storeys were not less than forty feet, but were loosened by frost in 1739.

If a tower forty feet high were placed on this mound then the total height would be 80 feet. It would not be possible to see the 'hills of Somerset', but this could be interpreted as a confusion with the hills of Glamorgan.

The Great Mound, Caerleon

Primrose Hockey in her book *Caerleon Past and Present* tells of a Caerleon man who had an amazing adventure:

'Wending his way down Mill Street, after a night out at the Red Lion, he was amazed to hear sounds of music and revelry coming from the direction of the Mound. Being curious he went to investigae only to be arrested by a soldier wearing an ancient type of uniform. He was led to where a great iron doorway led into the Mound. He was welcomed by men in armour and bidden to partake of the excellent food and wine with which the tables were laden. On the tables were also heaps of gold and silver. To his amazement he discovered that he was sitting at a table with King Arthur and his Knights and was made to feel quite at home. When he had had enough he decided to leave and he was given a bag of gold coins and bade 'God Speed' when he left. In the morning he was found lying dead drunk by the roadside near to the Mynde. Although he had no gold on him, he insisted that his story was true. He became teetotal and to the day of his death persisted in telling his story.'

Tradition says that the tower was of such a height that from its summit it was possible to see over Christchurch hill to the Bristol Channel beyond. This would have made it higher than the Post Office Tower in London!

THE FORTRESS ON THE HILL

It is of considerable interest that to the north west of Caerleon is the South Wales equivalent of the West Country's Cadbury Castle, for on the highest part of Lodge Hill, overlooking a curve of the River Usk is a large fort which was occupied by the Silures at the time of the Roman invasion.

The fort is 119 metres above sea level and consists of a main enclosure of a flattenened oval outline, which is protected by three massive ramparts and ditches which in some places are 10 metres deep. The whole camp measure 440 metres long and has an average width of 175 metres. It is situated at the highest point of a ridge which stretches between Malpas and Caerleon and provides a panoramic view of the surrounding area.

Geoffrey of Monmouth associated this fort with King Belinus the son of Dyfnwal Moelmud who is said to have ruled this area jointly with his brother Bran. He tells us that: *Belinus returned to Britain, which he governed for the remainder of his life in peace. Cities (hill forts?) that were falling into ruin he repaired, and built many new ones. Among the rest he built one upon the River Uske, near the Severn Sea, which was for a long time called Caerosc, and was the metropolis of Demetia; but after the coming of the Romans it lost its first name and was called the City of the Legions which used to take up their winter quarters in it.*

Beli, Belin or Belinus is also credited with building the city of Bristol and his effigy can be seen on St John's Church, Broad Street, Bristol. There is a tradition that he also constructed several roads, one of which came from the direction of Caerwent and forded the Usk to Caerleon.

When the Romans approached 'Belinstocke' (Stronghold of Belin) in the 1st century it would have been strongly defended by the British forces and such a fort was almost impregnable for an attacking force. Its ramparts were 4 - 5 metres high and the north side plunged deeply towards the valley. The original entrance to the fort is on the south east side with an additional rampart to strengthen it.

Eventually Belinstock fell to the Romans and they were able to establish a chain of camps in Gwent which effectively brought the Silures into subjection. The Romans used this hill top citadel as a summer camp and constructed a road up to it from the North Gate of Isca to provide easy access. On the southern side of the hill runs the old Roman road known as the Via Julia which connected Bath with Carmarthen.

This magnificent hill fort on Lodge Hill has never been excavated, even though it is probably as important as Cadbury Castle in Somerset and could very well reveal evidence of Dark Age occupation. Unfortunately the Roman fort of Isca continues to claim the archaeologists' attention and all the available financial resources for excavation.

Encampment of the Lodge

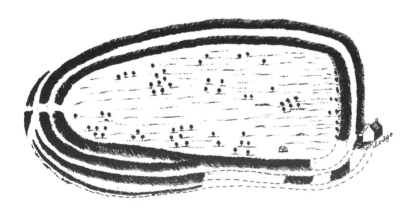

THE MAGIC MANTLE

The ancient romances describe many interesting incidents that took place at Caerleon. Take the days when Arthur's Court met here in high festivity and one day came to this place the mysterious 'Boy,' who brought the 'Magic Mantle,' and opened its lustrous folds wide to the amazing gaze of the Queen and her ladies. Nothing so fair and brilliant had ever been worn on mortal shoulders. Everyone of the ladies prersent longed to possess it. It was not for sale, but the Boy would give it if any lady present could wear it, and again he shook the glittering samite in the sunshine. "If any could wear it?' What a ridiculous proviso! Each one prided herself on the slope of her shoulders, and held forth her hand.

'Beauty of shape is not all that is required,' said the lad, with a mischievous twinkling in his eye: 'I warn ye that this garment can be worn by none but a lady of the strictest virtues.'

How was this? The eager hands were withdrawn, but only for a few minutes. Then there came the thought, 'Our secrets are known to none but ourselves.' 'Let me try it,' said the wife of one of the proudest knights. 'Take it,' said the Boy; but no sooner had the lady flung it over her shoulders, than it began to warp and wrinkle in the strangest manner. Tug at it how she would, it would not 'sit,' and, crimson with shame, she flung down the mantle and hid herself behind her sister-hood. The other knights were each confident of their wives good behaviour, and each one pushed his lady forward. One after another the dames undertook the test and each like the first, found she could not weat the confounded thing. Then the King commanded that the Queen should take it. She did so, but no sooner had she donned it than it shrank up to her very neck. All the fair ones were discomfited and angry. No, not all; there yet remained one, the beautiful Tegan, wife of Sir Caradoc Fraichfras. 'Go forth,' said her husband, 'and try thy fortune in thy tur,' How she fared is told in the words of the old bal-lad:-

'The lady, gently blushing, with modest step came on,
And now to try the mantle courageously had gone.
When she had taken the mantle, and put it on her back,
About the hem it seemed to wrinkle and to crack,
Lie still, she cried, O mantle, and shame me not for naught;
I'll freely own whate'er amiss or baneful I have wrought
Once I kissed Sir Caradoc beneath the greenwood tree;
Once I kissed Sir Caradoc before he married me.
When thus she had her shriven, and her worst fault had told,
The mantle soon became her right comely as it should. '

The mantle was hers. Then the Boy produced a magic knife, with which none but Sir Caradoc could carve the boar's head set on the table before the king.

Sir Caradoc was Lord of Brecon as well as of the Land of Ferlex, which lay between the confluence of the Severn and the Wye. His wife, the inimitable Tegan, was a Gwent lady, daughter of King Pelinor. Many of the leading families of this area claim to have inher-ited the blood of this illustrious pair!

KING ARTHUR SLEEPS IN A CAERLEON CAVE!

Caerleon's Arthurian associations certainly cover many aspects of the traditional story for there is even said to be a secret cave in this locality where Arthur and his men are sleeping in readiness to be called upon to rise once more to the aid of their country in a time of great danger.

One version of the legend concerns a farmer who met a man on horseback wearing a three-cornered hat. He offered to show him something amazing. They went to the middle of a wood and the man dismounted from his horse and moved a large boulder to reveal the mouth of a cave. They entered and followed a passage for some distance until they reached a flight of steps, above which hung two bells. The farmer was warned not to touch them. Descending the steps the two men entered a large cavern where one thousand soldiers lay sleeping. The guide told the farmer that these were the soldiers of Arthur and pointed to the king himself at their head.

On returning up the steps the farmer accidently knocked one of the bells and the loud clang that it made awoke the soldiers who in unison asked 'Is it time yet?' 'No not yet replied the guide - go back to sleep!' The soldiers obediently lay down and the two men made their way out of the cave. In later years the farmer often searched for the cave entrance but failed to find it.

ARTHURIAN ASSOCIATIONS
IN THE VICINITY OF CAERLEON

There are numerous little churches and other features in the Caerleon area that can be shown to have links with the time of King Arthur. These connections are part of a jig saw puzzle that provides an entangled web of legend and history. For example:-

Llandegfedd was once known as Llan Degwed and is dedicated to St Tegfedd first married Cedig ap Ceredig ap Cunedda by whom she became the mother of Afan of Bualth and then Enllyn ap Hydwy ap Credig by whom she had a child named Teilo who is well remebered as one of the Bishops of Llandaff. Llandegfedd church is built on the spot where she was murdered and it used to be known as Merthyr Tegfedd.

Llanderfil was a chapel in the adjoining parish of Llanfihangel juxta Llantarnam. It used to be known as St Derfil's Church and belonged to the Cistercian Abbey of Caerleon. Rice Davies in his 'Essay on the Welsh Saints' ascribes it to Derfel Gadarn (Derfel the Strong) who fought with Arthur at the battle of Camlan. Towards the end of his life he gave up his warlike ways and turned to religion.

Llangybi, half-way between Caerleon and Usk was founded by Cybi the son of Selyf, son of Geraint - who was killed at the battle of Llongborth. Cybi was a cousin of Dewi (St. David) and he was present at the famous Synod held at Llandewi Brefi.

Llandewi Fach, just north of Caerleon is dedicated to Dewi (David) who tradition tells us was the uncle of King Arthur.

Llanbadoc, near Usk, in ancient times was known as Cil Feignan 'Meignant's Retreat'. He was the son of Gwyndaf Hen ap Emyr Llydaw by Gwenonwy, daughter of Meurig ap Tewdrig.

41

Llanfrechfa, to the west of Caerleon is said to be named after Caradoc Freichfras (Strong Arm) who according to the Welsh Triads was Arthur's Chief Elder at Gelliwig. His grandson was Medraut who died fighting Arthur at Camlan.

Llechau occurs as the name of a stream near Caerleon and this name corresponds to Llacheu, a son of Arthur. The *'Vulgate Merlin '* makes Llacheu an illegitimate son of Arthur by Lissonar, the daughter of Earl Sevain of Castle Quimper-Corentin in Brittanny.

Catsash, on the ridge above Caerleon beside the ancient Via Julia, is the site of an ancient chapel dedicated to St Curig who is said to have been one of Arthur's soldiers.

Yes, there certainly are some fascinating Arthurian connections in the Caerleon area, apart from those which are mainly of a legendary and literary origin and an intricate and fascinating web of such connections can be found throughout Wales.

One man who is convinced that Caerleon is the true site of Arthur's fabulous court of Camelot is Dr Russell Rhys who has established a visitor centre called the Ffwrm where an Arthurian sculpture garden has become a very popular attraction. He has had thrones carved from solid elm for Arthur and Guinevere, portraying the faces and figures of the King and Queen, the knights and Merlin the Wizard. They wreath in and out of the carved designs emphasising their elusive nature. It is Dr Rhys's intention to have seats carved for all the significant members of the Round Table as a token of his own faith in Caerleon's claim to be the site of Arthur's Court.

We will leave the last word to Lady Charlotte Guest, who visited Caerleon on 19 January, 1842 and later wrote in her diary:

'While in the eddying stream of life we pause to look back upon the days when Caerleon and its Round Table formed to us an ideal world, we feel that, in our hearts at least, 'King Arthur is not dead.'

SUGGESTED READING

Alcock, Leslie, *Arthur's Britain* (Allen Lane, London 1971).

Ashe, Geoffrey (Editor), *The Quest for Arthur's Britain* (Paladin 1968).

Bromwich, Rachel *Trioedd ynys Prydein - The Welsh Triads* (University of Wales 1961.)

Chambers, E.K., *Arthur of Britain* (Sidgwick 1927).

The Mabinogion, Tran. Guest, Lady Charlotte (John Jones, Cardiff).

Fairbairn, Neil, *Kingdoms of Arthur* (Evans Brothers 1983).

Geoffrey of Monmouth, *The History of the Kings of Britain*, (Trans., Thorpe, L., Penguin)

Giraldus Cambrensis, *The Historical Works*, trans., Wright, T., Bohn, G., 1863.

Lacy, Norris, J., *The Arthurian Encycolpedia* (The Boydell Press 1988).

Malory, Sir Thomas, *Le Morte d" Arthur* (Penguin 1969).

Marsh, Henry *Dark Age Britain* (David & Charles 1970).

Morris, John *The Age of Arthur* (Weidenfeld & Nicholson 1971).

Nennius, *History of the Britons* trans. John Morris (Phillimore 1980.

PUBLICATIONS BY BLORENGE BOOKS

Blorenge Books publish books about Wales and in particular the area covered by the ancient kingdom of Gwent. This is the first booklet to be published about King Arthur and more are planned for the future.

Copies of the following titles may be obtained by writing to Blorenge Books and enclosing cheques (made out to Blorenge Books) for the relevant amounts:-

Hando's Gwent Volume II by Chris Barber......................................£7.50

The Ancient Stones of Wales by Chris Barber and John Williams....£7.95

Journey to Avalon by Chris Barber & David Pykitt............................£9.90

The Seven Hills of Abergavenny by Chris Barber.......................... £5.25

Please add on £1 for postage and packing

Blorenge Books, Blorenge Cottage, Church Lane, Llanfoist
Abergavenny NP7 9NG
Tel: 01873 856114

Journey to Avalon
The Final Discovery of King Arthur

To learn more about King Arthur you should read Journey to Avalon by Chris Barber & David Pykitt. This fascinating book sorts out fact from fiction to provide the most convincing and detailed account of King Arthur and his times that has ever been compiled. Packed with illustrations and intriguing information, it is a work of historical detection in which a solution is given to one of the greatest mysteries in the world.

The true identity of Arthur, the sixth-century King of the Britons is explained and also the location of his courts and long forgotten battle sites such as Badon and Camlan. The authors also reveal the secret of the mysterious Isle of Avalon and the location of Arthur's tomb in a Breton church.

Through their intensive research the authors have found that King Henry VII in fact knew the identity of King Arthur, but an academic muddle has obscured the truth of the matter and as a result this Dark Age king has become the subject of fiction and fantasy.

This fascinating book explains the importance of the links between South Wales, Cornwall and Brittany, providing the reasons why King Arthur is so well remembered in those areas. Fact is sometimes more remarkable than fiction and this intriguing book has been eagerly sought by people in many parts of the world who wish to know the truth about King Arthur.

Published by Blorenge Books, Blorenge Cottage, Church Lane, Llanfoist,
Abergavenny, Gwent NP7 9NG.
@ £9.99.
Tel : 01873 856114.